Presented with deepest sympathy
to

_____

from

_____

date

_____

THE Comfort BOOK

for Those Who Mourn

Compiled by Anna Trimiew

Harold Shaw Publishers
Wheaton, Illinois

We have sought to secure permissions for all copyrighted material in this book. Where copyright holders could not be located or acknowledgment was inadvertently omitted, the publisher expresses its regret.

All Scripture quotations, unless otherwise indicated, are taken from the HOLY BIBLE, NEW INTERNATIONAL VERSION®. NIV®. Copyright © 1973, 1978, 1984 by International Bible Society. Used by permission of Zondervan Publishing House. All rights reserved.

Scriptures marked *KJV* are taken from the King James Version of the Bible. Scriptures marked *RSV* are taken from the Revised Standard Version of the Bible, © 1946, 1952, 1971 by the Division of Christian Education of the National Council of Churches of Christ in the USA. Used by permission. Scripture marked *TLB* are taken from *The Living Bible* © 1971. Used by permission of Tyndale House Publishers, Inc., Wheaton, IL 60189. All rights reserved.

Cover design by David LaPlaca
Compiled by Anna Trimiew

ISBN 0-87788-136-7

Library of Congress Cataloging-in-Publication Data

The comfort book for those who mourn / compiled by Anna Trimiew.
    p. cm.
  ISBN 0-87788-136-7
  1. Consolation—Prayer-books and devotions—English. 2. Consolation—Biblical teaching. 3. Grief—Biblical teaching. 4. Bereavement—Religious aspects—Christianity. I. Trimiew, Anna, 1948-
BV4909.C65 1996
242'.4—dc20
                                            96-26385
                                              CIP

02 01 00 99 98

10 9 8 7 6 5 4 3 2

WORDS TO COMFORT YOU

Facing the Unknown

Grieving

Consolation and Inspiration

The Journey to Recovery

FACING THE UNKNOWN

Coming to Terms with Dying

We don't think about death a lot, do we? Nor should we. Instead, we go about the business of living, making plans, falling in love, getting married, having children, beginning careers, in short, making the most of what life has to offer, and not dwelling too much on its ending.

It takes only a fraction of a second to shatter that sense of well-being—a brief moment when we have an accident, or an instant when a blood clot forms in a loved one's aorta. When such an event happens, the world we knew suddenly seems to vanish, and suddenly we see ourselves as the vulnerable creatures we always knew we were but somehow never fully acknowledged.

Helen Fitzgerald, The Mourning Handbook

He who would teach men to die would teach them to live.

Michel Montaigne, Essays

Isaac said, "I am now an old man and don't know the day of my death."

Genesis 27:2

When I was a little boy, eight years old I think, I realized one day that I was going to die sometime. What a terrible moment that was. Everything in the whole world seemed to crack and crumble. Nothing meant anything anymore. How could I ever be happy again, knowing that death was somewhere out there in the future waiting for me?

Buff Bradley, Endings

I think of death as a glad awakening from this troubled sleep which we call life; as an emancipation from a world which, beautiful though it be, is still a land of captivity.

Lyman Abbott

Lord, grant that my last hour may be my best hour.

John Aubrey

I want death to find me planting my cabbages.

Michel Montaigne, Essays

And there it was. My death handed to me like a waiter's check. I looked it over and realized with surprise that I had not been staggered or dismayed at the amount of the bill. There was numbness and shock, but I felt no anger or self-pity. . . . Instead, I accepted the verdict with a calm that surprised me. Somehow, I had been prepared for it. Because Kay and I, in sharing her work, had talked about death so often, I was open to the news of its imminent visitation. Kay's ability to help her dying clients meet their death courageously had prepared me to accept my own.

Herbert and Kay Kramer, Conversations at Midnight

For everything there is a season, and a time for every matter under heaven: a time to be born, and a time to die.

Ecclesiastes 3:1-2, RSV

Death is not a period but a comma in the story of life.

Anonymous

I bequeath my soul to God. . . . My body to be buried obscurely. For my name and memory, I leave it to men's charitable speeches, and to foreign nations, and the next age.

Francis Bacon's will

Death is the side of life which is turned away from us.

Rainer Maria Rilke

The great attribute of heaven and earth is the giving and maintaining of life. While you do not know about life, how can you know about death?

Confucius

Soon-a will be done-a with the troubles of the world,
Troubles of the world,
The troubles of the world.
Soon-a will be done-a with the troubles of the world.
Goin' home to live with God.

Traditional

Death did not frighten Brother Lawrence at all. On his deathbed, he displayed marks of a stability, a resignation, and a joy that were quite extraordinary.

Joseph de Beaufort, in The Practice of the Presence of God

The bed of sickness is not the proper place to examine the evidences of religion; it is not the place to make preparations for death; not the proper place to become religious. Religion demands the best vigour of the intellect and the calmest state of the heart; and this great subject should be

SETTLED in our minds before we are sick—before we are laid on the bed of death.

C. S. Lewis, A Grief Observed

There are, in fact, times when God must strip us of things or persons we rely on in order to remind us that He is our real life and hope.

E. Calvin Beisner, Psalms of Promise

My flesh and my heart faileth: but God is the strength of my heart, and my portion for ever.

Psalm 73:26, KJV

Why Is This So Hard?

Fear threatens to overwhelm faith.

John White, The Fight

It is no coincidence that the despised villain of one of our most popular mythologies, the Star Wars trilogy, is named Darth Vader, or Death, the Invader.

Herbert and Kay Kramer, Conversations at Midnight

The last enemy that shall be destroyed is death.

1 Corinthians 15:26, KJV

Even such is Time, that takes in trust
Our youth, our joys, our all we have,
And pays us but with earth and dust;
Who in the dark and silent grave,
when we have wandered all our ways
Shuts up the story of our days;

But from this earth, this grave, this dust,
My God shall raise me up, I trust.

Written on the fly-leaf of Sir Walter Raleigh's Bible

There's a special brand of grieving that begins with a terminal prognosis that inexorably, incrementally, becomes reality. . . . Anticipated death is a shared process, a delicate improvised dance of perpetual imbalance in which partners alternately hold each other up and allow each other to let go. For the person who is ill, fear of death is complicated by its practical embarrassments. For the eventual survivor, impending loss is regularly made worse by exhaustion and frustration. Yet when this pas de deux is performed with dignity and—there's no other word for it—style, no human act is braver or more ennobling.

Michael Dorris, in Grieving, *by Ruth Coughlin*

The event of death is always astounding; our philosophy never reaches, never possesses it; we are always at the beginning of our catechism; always the definition is yet to be made. What is death?

Ralph Waldo Emerson

First there was the death of my mother, from cancer, when I was twenty-two. Only the year before, while still a college senior, I helped my boy-friend, Peter (now my husband), through his own bout with radical can-cer surgery, radiation treatments, and chemotherapy. Coming one on top of the other, these battles—one successful, the other not—left me raw and numb, utterly weary, but perhaps, I hoped, also a little bit wise.

Diane Cole, After Great Pain

Men fear death as children fear to go in the dark; and as that natural fear in children is increased with tales, so is the other.

Francis Bacon

The length of our days is seventy years—
or eighty, if we have the strength;
yet their span is but trouble and sorrow,
for they quickly pass, and we fly away.

Psalm 90:10

When your baby dies, you never get the chance to know the baby in the way that we normally think of knowing someone. But your hopes and dreams for this child have already become part of your life. You have not only lost a child, you have lost the chance to see your baby grow, become a vital part of the family and realize his or her potential. Your baby's death represents a deeply felt loss of a wished-for child, as well as a loss of your fantasies, hopes and dreams. Indeed, it represents a denial of part of your future, part of yourself.

Deborah L. Davis, Empty Cradle, Broken Heart

The wailing of the newborn infant is mingled with the dirge for the dead.

Lucretius

Death has but one terror—that it has no tomorrow.

Eric Hoffer, The True Believer

Keeping from going over the edge may well rest on our preparing for troubles before they come. The practice of constant prayer, self-denial, and thankfulness must become ingrained before we encounter desperate hardship, lest we meet the enemy unprepared.

E. Calvin Beisner, Psalms of Promise

What a man believes about immortality will color his thinking in every area of life.

John Sutherland Bonnell

Life is a series of surprises, and would not be worth taking or keeping if it were not.

Ralph Waldo Emerson

I was catapulted into a new life when my husband died, a life for which I was totally unprepared, even though Martin and I had known for fourteen months that he was going to die. . . .

After a few weeks of blessed numbness, feeling crept back. Martin had died, but I had been transported to hell. My grief was a raw wound that would not heal. But grief was only part of it. I was desperately frightened and confused, panicky, angry, lost.

Lynn Caine, Lifelines

No one can tell you about grief, about its limitless boundaries, its unfathomable depths. No one can tell you about the crater that is created in the center of your body, the one that nothing can fill. No matter how many times you hear the word *final,* it means nothing until final is actually final.

Ruth Coughlin, Grieving

The beginnings and endings of all human undertakings are untidy.

John Galsworthy

There are only two or three human stories, and they go on repeating themselves as fiercely as if they had never happened.

Willa Cather, O Pioneers!

Our mother's prolonged illness and death is a horrifying portion of our family story. We watched as our capable and vivacious mother gradually became fearful, trembling, confused, and bedridden. Throughout the course of her strange illness, she saw several doctors, and dutifully downed hundreds of pills, all the while becoming more vacant and isolated. We knew that she had Parkinson's and some form of early-onset dementia. But without ever having consistent or clear medical guidance, our family stumbled through her illness and care, not always knowing what to do or how to attend to her needs.

When she died, we were already in mourning—had been for several years. There were uneasy feelings of guilt, relief, and a profound sense of loss. The mother I knew and cherished had quietly vanished years before.

Anonymous

Saying Good-bye

This shall be my parting word—know what you want to do—then do it. Make straight for your goal and go undefeated in spirit to the end.

Ernestine Schumann-Heink, in Schumann-Heink, the Last of the Titans, *by Mary Lawton*

God, who dost punish sin and willingly forgive, I have loved this people. That I have borne its shame and burdens, and seen its salvation—that is enough. Seize me and hold me! My staff is sinking; O faithful God, prepare my grave.

Deitrich Bonhoeffer, Letters and Papers from Prison

For each of us there comes a moment when death takes us by the hand and says—it is time to rest, you are tired, lie down and sleep.

On Will Hay's tombstone, taken from the last book he read

He was given some final time alone to reflect on the great grace which God had given him during his life. When asked how he spent that time, he replied that he had been doing what he would be doing for all eternity—"Blessing God, praising God, adoring him, and loving him with all my heart. That is our whole purpose, brothers, to adore God and to love him, without worrying about the rest."

The next day, February 12th, 1691, without any agony and without the loss of any of his senses, Brother Lawrence of the Resurrection died in the embrace of the Lord.

Joseph de Beaufort, in The Practice of the Presence of God

So Moses, the disciple of the Lord, died in the land of Moab as the Lord had said. The Lord buried him in a valley near Beth-Peor in Moab, but no one knows the exact place.

Moses was 120 years old when he died, yet his eyesight was perfect and he was as strong as a young man. The people of Israel mourned for him for thirty days on the plains of Moab.

Deuteronomy 34:5-8, TLB

A strange providence of God, it may seem to us, that Oswald Chambers should conclude his ministry on earth while still in his forties; but the ways of Him who knoweth best are past finding out.

V. Raymond Edman, They Found the Secret

As they were walking along and talking together, suddenly a chariot of fire and horses of fire appeared and separated the two of them, and Elijah went up to heaven in a whirlwind. Elisha saw this and cried out, "My father! My father! The chariots and horsemen of Israel!" And Elisha saw him no more.

2 Kings 2:11-12

In the morning, Doug was quieter than usual, but otherwise fine. Everyone arrived; each family member spent time with him. Just before noon Doug was lying in bed, talking with his mother. He suddenly became restless, saying he wasn't comfortable, then sat up and asked his mother to rearrange his pillows. He seemed to be having trouble breathing. Then he lay back, closed his eyes, and died.

When I arrived to confirm his death, I asked his mother, "He knew this was going to happen, didn't he?"

She handed me a piece of paper on which Doug had drawn a diagram of a football play. . . . The circle that bore Doug's initials had an arrow that went across the line and out of bounds: beside it he had scribbled, "Out of the game by noon on Sunday."

"Maybe when you're close to dying you know more about death than anyone else," his father said. "I'm so glad that he told us with that diagram."

Maggie Callanan & Patricia Kelley, Final Gifts

And as the murderous stones came hurtling at him, Stephen prayed, "Lord Jesus, receive my spirit." And he fell to his knees, shouting, "Lord, don't charge them with this sin!" and with that, he died.

Acts 7:59-60, TLB

I spent most of the afternoon holding her, and then they withdrew life-support systems, disconnected everything, and we held her again. It was so sad, but I'm really glad we were able to hold her as much as we did. I think maybe it helped her a little bit; at least she had us there to hold her.

Hannah, in Empty Cradle, Broken Heart, *by Deborah L. Davis*

Earlier in the evening on the night Kelly died, she said to her mother, "Mommy, I want to go home."

"But you are home, honey," my sister tenderly told her.

"No, I want to go home with Jesus," she whispered hoarsely. Within several hours she was there. Kelly passed away surrounded in bed by her family, stuffed animals, and a suitcase packed with her jeans, dresses, and toys.

Joni Eareckson Tada, When Is It Right to Die?

Her death came one day after Ronnie and Sharon's first wedding anniversary; she had called to wish them happiness. And so she had seen all her children launched and settled. In the weeks and month before, she had also, to the best of her ability, arranged for the care of her aged parents and her reclusive sister in Cleveland. She had done what she wanted that year, and she had died in dignity, in her own bed at home. She was not an unfinished woman, and she had not led an unfinished life.

Diane Cole, After Great Pain

It was "hallelujah!" all the way, even to [Samuel Logan Brengle's] last murmured words . . . for the holiness of God flooded his life. Since that meeting of the Savior in seminary days there had continued with him the unfailing Presence, the preciousness of God's salvation, and the power of His Spirit, with perseverance to the end: and all because of purification of heart.

Edman, They Found the Secret

That day a man named Simeon, a Jerusalem resident, was in the Temple. He was a good man, very devout, filled with the Holy Spirit and constantly expecting the Messiah to come soon. For the Holy Spirit had revealed to him that he would not die until he had seen him—God's anointed King. The Holy Spirit had impelled him to go to the Temple that day; and so, when Mary and Joseph arrived to present the baby

Jesus to the Lord in obedience to the law, Simeon was there and took the child in his arms, praising God.

"Lord," he said, "now I can die content! For I have seen him as you promised me I would."

Luke 2:25-30, TLB

When it came, she was ready for the end. I am convinced of that and grateful for it. But though we knew the end was near, we also refused to know and were not prepared. For the living, death always comes as a shock, no matter how long or certain the knowledge that what is coming will come. . . . The music was my way of saying good-bye to her. I could not actually say the word *good-bye*.

Diane Cole, After Great Pain

The Valley of the Shadow

When we see death, if we see it at all, it comes to us from outside. "I'm only twenty-two. Why should anyone do this to me?" Jeanette cried when she first learned she had multiple sclerosis.

Judith Ahronheim, M.D., and Doron Weber, Final Passages

You gain strength, courage, and confidence by every experience in which you really stop to look fear in the face.

Eleanor Roosevelt, You Learn by Living

Even though I walk through the valley of the shadow of death,
I will fear no evil, for you are with me;
your rod and your staff, they comfort me.

Psalm 23:4

Everything has its wonders, even darkness and silence, and I learn, whatever state I may be in, therein to be content.

Helen Keller, The Story of My Life

In the hour of adversity be not without hope
For crystal rain falls from black clouds.

Nizami

Every time we breathe someone is dying. We all know that we are going to
stay here but a very little while. Our life is but a vapor. It is only a shadow.

Dwight L. Moody, Heaven

The fog is rising.

Emily Dickinson's last words

Sadness and despair can be excruciatingly painful. These feelings can
make you feel broken, discouraged and overwhelmed. You may be afraid
that if you start crying, you may never stop. But, in fact, you may notice
that if you really take the time and energy to cry, to think about your . . .
loss, to really feel the pain, then you can also feel relief from holding
these powerful emotions inside.

Deborah L. Davis, Empty Cradle, Broken Heart

I felt truly alone in the world. I could hear the world—traffic humming
along the avenue, the elevator clanking and groaning, a telephone ring-

ing. My telephone. But I didn't move. Let the world go its way. I was getting off. Tears were trickling down my cheeks. I had tried. I had tried so hard. I had run everywhere, done everything. But the more I did, the worse things got. Nothing worked out the way it should. I started crying in earnest.

Lynn Caine, Lifelines

Lord, help me.

Matthew 15:25

Grief is unpredictable and largely uncontrollable, showing us a side of ourselves we didn't know was there. It can be terrifying and unnerving.

Helen Fitzgerald, The Mourning Handbook

Suffering passes, but the fact of having suffered never leaves us.

Leon Bloy

Let us cross over the river and rest under the shade of the trees.

General Thomas Jackson

When the undertaker came for his body later in the morning, he asked if we wanted to leave the room while the body was prepared for removal. Remarkably, the children and I answered in unison, "No." We stood vigil. When it was time for him to leave, each one of us gave him a farewell kiss. We accompanied his body out the door and onto the porch, where we all watched in silence as the hearse drove off down the street.

Herbert and Kay Kramer, Conversations at Midnight

People . . . fear death because they don't know what it is. They are afraid of the unknown. Maybe death is not-being, maybe it's something that's unspeakably horrible.

Buff Bradley, Endings

When someone you love is facing death, what can you do? Face it together and do what you can.

Ted Menten, Gentle Closings

You will not fear the terror of night,
  nor the arrow that flies by day,
nor the pestilence that stalks in the darkness,
  nor the plague that destroys at midday.

Psalm 91:5-6

The waters are rising, but I am not sinking.

Catherine Booth's last words

Slowly, I emerged from the abyss of terror. I lived through the seasons of grief, none of which can be denied if we are to emerge on its other side.

Lynn Caine, Lifelines

Bring us, O Lord God,
at our last awakening into the house and gate of heaven,
to enter into that gate and dwell in that house,
where there shall be no darkness nor dazzling,
but one equal light;
no noise nor silence,
but one equal music;
no fears nor hopes,
but one equal possession;
no ends nor beginnings,
but one equal eternity;
in the habitations of thy glory and dominion world without end.

John Donne

GRIEVING

The Power of Emotions

If you are caught up in the emotions of grief, I don't have to tell you what they are like. They are all-consuming. . . . One stricken mother, mourning the death of her son, told me she could not understand why the birds continued to sing or the sun continued to rise in the morning.

Helen Fitzgerald, The Mourning Handbook

The idea of dying can be very worrying. Some people try to ignore the whole subject of death. It is as if they feel that if they do not talk about it, it will not happen to them. Sometimes the fears we have can seem less threatening if we just try to understand them.

Pete Sanders, Death and Dying

The fear of death is more to be dreaded than death.

Publius Syrus

There is the matter of loneliness, that aching realization which comes upon you in so many different ways and reminds you that someone you shared lives with is no longer about. The simple delights of showing off the new coat you bought, of going to a movie and discussing it afterward, of telling about some small success in life, are gone. If it is a beloved spouse who died, there is no harsher reminder of your loss than facing an empty bed each evening.

Martin Shepard, M.D., Someone You Love Is Dying

Death may be the greatest of all human blessings.

Socrates

She died peacefully, in the certitude that death was not a calamity.

Survivor of Belsen, describing the death of Anne Frank

Help us to hope that the seeming Shadow of this Death is to our human blindness but the exceeding brightness of a newer greater life.

W. E. B. Du Bois, Prayers for Dark People

Death, no matter how we plan for it, is still the last outrage. But we can make dying as peaceable and serene as possible. You actually can go through death in peace, even serenity. It all depends on the way you view life.

Joni Eareckson Tada, When Is It Right to Die?

Your outlook on life is a conscious choice.

Susan Murray Young

I felt that I had found an acceptable prayer to pray, and in the silence and stillness I was even, for a moment, prepared to believe it possible that my tears were a token of the "loving-kindness of the heart of our God," who gives "light to those in darkness."

John Cornwell, The Hiding Place of God

The forces that would kill on the stormy landscape of the frightened heart do not, after all, have the last word.

Martin E. Marty, A Cry of Absence

The Lord is close to the brokenhearted
  and saves those who are crushed in spirit.

Psalm 34:18

Intense emotions hit you when you least expect them. . . . Anger and even rage are common reactions to the loss of a loved one.

Helen Fitzgerald, The Mourning Handbook

Emma felt anger creep up the back of her neck: anger at her parents for bringing Aunt Sue into her quiet healthy home, anger at Aunt Sue for being sick, anger at the doctors for not making her well, and even anger at God—a God who was supposed to love them, but who was going to let Aunt Sue die anyway.

Carolyn Nystrom, Emma Says Goodbye

Integrating the awareness of death and the living out of remaining time is not the easiest of tasks. It is ultimately an individual trip, for no companion may join the dying person. The traveler typically traverses landscapes fraught with emotional turmoil before finding ultimate peace and acceptance.

Martin Shepard, Someone You Love Is Dying

The only way out is ahead, and our choice is whether we shall cringe from it or affirm it.

Rollo May

To lose a child is the most awful, agonizing, horrible grief; it breaks your heart forever, an unbearable pain that scars the soul. Nothing can change that reality. Never can there be a time of greater despair or helplessness, no matter how strong your faith or how courageous you are.

Alexandra Stoddard, Making Choices

Lord, I am hurting right now, to the point of numbness. The only comfort I truly have at this moment is knowing that you are gently holding me in your arms. It makes me realize that you have always been faithful to get me through the storms. This gives me the confidence and comfort to carry on.

Charles Stanley, A Touch of His Love

The best prayers have often more groans than words.

John Bunyan

Blessed are they that mourn: for they shall be comforted.

Matthew 5:4, KJV

Grief is more than just feeling sad. No two people grieve or react to a death in the same way. In fact people who are grieving may be surprised or confused by all their different reactions. You may feel lost and unsure about what to do.

Pete Sanders, Death and Dying

An Uneven Life

Finally, with one last, long sigh, Bobby died. As we sat—holding him and one another—Bill said that, when I had gone to get the medicine, Bobby had spoken clearly for the first time in more than three days.

"He told us, 'I can see the light down the road, and it's beautiful,'" Bill said.

This glimpse of the other place gives immeasurable comfort to many, and often is perceived as a final gift from the one who died.

Maggie Callanan & Patricia Kelley, Final Gifts

We do not live an equal life, but one of contrasts and patchwork; now a little joy, then a sorrow, now a sin, then a generous or brave action.

Ralph Waldo Emerson

The cold of January blurred into the past. A house full of relatives, neighbors, and friends. A refrigerator packed with food brought by people who wanted to help. A casket with a spray of flowers on top and Aunt Sue inside looking asleep in her long-sleeved blue silk dress. Friends standing in front of the casket and crying. A funeral at church full of music and words from the Bible about living forever in heaven with Jesus, where people play and sing and dance and work, and no one ever, ever cries.

Carolyn Nystrom, Emma Says Goodbye

Between grief and nothing I will take grief.

William Faulkner

Tragedies don't go away by denial.

Alexandra Stoddard, Making Choices

I asked a group of children what they thought was going to happen when they died. Going to heaven was a popular destination.
"How will you get there?" I asked.
"An angel will come and get me," replied Wendy.
"Beamed up like on 'Star Trek,'" said Bobby.
"I want Lassie to take me," said little Sharon.
"But Lassie's only a dog!" said a disapproving Bobby.
"I know, but Lassie always knows how to get home."

Ted Menten, Gentle Closings

We thank Thee, O Lord, for the gift of Death—for the great silence that follows the jarring noises of the world—the rest that is Peace. We who live to see the passing of that fine and simple Old Man, who has so often sat beside us here in this room, must not forget the legacy he leaves us or the Hope he still holds to us: we are richer for his sacrifice, truer for his honesty and better for his goodness. And his living leaves us firm in the faith that the kingdom of heaven will yet reign among men.

W. E. B. Du Bois, Prayers for Dark People

Relying on God has to begin all over again every day as if nothing had yet been done.

C. S. Lewis

At this, Job got up and tore his robe and shaved his head. Then he fell to the ground in worship and said:
"Naked I came from my mother's womb,
and naked I will depart.
The Lord gave and the Lord has taken away;
may the name of the Lord be praised."

Job 1:20-21

God is the master of the scenes; we must not choose what part we shall act; it concerns us only to be careful that we do it well, always saying, "If this please God, let it be as it is."

Jeremy Taylor

Sudden deaths do not provide planning periods.

Dr. Catherine M. Sanders, Surviving Grief

There are no right and wrongs for grief work . . . grief is a process.

Sandra L. Graves, in What to Do When a Loved One Dies *by Eva Shaw*

Her son was dead, killed in a tragic accident only a few days before. She sat in the front pew of the church, listening quietly as the minister spoke at the memorial service, her face composed, one might almost say serene. When the final prayer ended, friends filed by the casket, hugging members of the family through tears. Later it was said, "They are taking it so well." "His mother is a real brick." At the home afterward, the parents greeted dozens of people with smiles and words of encouragement.

A few days later her husband found his wife sitting on the kitchen floor, banging her fists and sobbing uncontrollably. The woman others thought was "so brave" was sick to the core of her being with an emotion common to every living person.

Billy Graham, Facing Death—and the Life After

Everyone who loves is vulnerable to the pain of grief, for love means attachment, and all human attachments are subject to loss. But grief need not, should not, be a destructive emotion.

Dr. Joyce Brothers, in What to Do When a Loved One Dies, *by Eva Shaw*

The past few months have been a time of ice without as well as ice within, and now the thaw had come. There was promise in the air. It was spring. I felt ready to move more decisively out of depression and loneliness, to reach out in new directions.

Lynn Caine, Lifelines

Facts call us to reflect, even as the tossings of a capsizing vessel cause the crew to rush on deck and to climb the masts.

Albert Schweitzer

People have . . . been known to feel relieved when somebody has died, particularly after a long illness. Others may be in shock, and for a time may not believe that the person has died. They might keep the dead person's room looking the same, or talk about the person as if he or she were still there. Often people might look brave and appear able to cope with their loss. You may think they have accepted the death, but they may just be numb and not able to let their real feelings show.

Pete Sanders, Death and Dying

They that love beyond the world cannot be separated by it. Death is but a crossing the world, as friends do the seas; they live in one another still.

William Penn

I came from God, and I'm going back to God, and I won't have any gaps of death in the middle of my life.

George MacDonald

Life is eternal; and love is immortal; and death is only a horizon; and a horizon is nothing save the limit of our sight.

Rossiter Worthington Raymond

Unexpected Reminders

After a personal loss, nothing looks the same. Food loses its flavor, music seems hollow, and nothing satisfies. Tears come at strange times, often for no apparent reason. The bereaved person may see someone walking down the street who looks like the person who died, and pain comes without warning.

Billy Graham, Facing Death—and the Life After

I caught my breath. The tall young man at the other end of the produce aisle looked so like my brother. The same lanky stoop, tousled blonde hair, and gentle face. Grateful for the warm, vivid reminder, I stared at the young man as he shopped for groceries. He turned towards me, and I looked away, suddenly feeling cold and starkly empty. This was not my brother. This "someone else" was just a pale, hollow imitation of my Stephen, who had died years before—killed instantly in a cruel car wreck.

Anonymous

It's natural to see signs and hear voices. Don't feel crazy, but be a little careful how you interpret them. Some people hang onto these signs as living proof that the one who died is still very near, physically. They want to believe that he or she is communicating with them from the other world and that our two worlds are very close together. A more healthy reading of signs is to see them as reminders that the love which was will always be.

Rev. Jack Silvey Miller, The Healing Power of Grief

Although I have taken it into my head that I cannot possibly sleep in our bed, I nevertheless proceed to conduct conversations with myself that go on for hours. *Don't be foolish,* I say, arguing against my original decision, *it's only a bed. You can do it. Toughen up. You don't need to stretch out, you can sleep on your side, just as you've been doing all these years.*

Ruth Coughlin, Grieving

No greater grief than to remember days of gladness when sorrow is at hand.

Friedrich Schiller

Only in winter can you tell which trees are truly green. Only when the winds of adversity blow can you tell whether an individual . . . has courage and steadfastness.

John F. Kennedy

Everyone can master grief but he that has it.

William Shakespeare

Leaning against the porch pillar, I wept as I remembered the sight of him the first time he appeared at this door.

Herbert and Kay Kramer, Conversations at Midnight

I hear myself in memory, weeping, and then I listen to my infant son erupt in tears as I take even one step to leave the room where he is playing. I think, The painful wail of the mourner is not so very different from the cries of children. It is only that, as adults, we recognize more fully than children the futility of hoping that our cries will bring the dead to life again or that an actual search will yield a similar recovery.

Diane Cole, After Great Pain

Mrs. Reiner had lived with her husband on a farm for all their married years. When he died, she found it comforting to put on one of her husband's old plaid shirts. She said it made her feel as though his arms were around her.

Dr. Catherine M. Sanders, Surviving Grief . . . & Learning to Live Again

If you cannot think clearly, seem forgetful, and seem detached, be patient with yourself. If you need help, ask for it.

Janice Harris Lord, No Time for Good-byes

We do not know where we are going, but we are on our way.

Stephen Vincent Benét

Look well into yourself: there is a source which will always spring up if you will search there.

Marcus Antonius

Feelings of loss are caused by feelings of love.

Margaret Edison, Living with AIDS

I believe in grief and sorrow and wailing and tears flowing like Niagara Falls. Tears mean something. They mean we're alive and feeling.

Ted Menten, Gentle Closings

I was just six years old when my sister, Heather, died of polio. The morning of her death my dad whispered in my ear that Heather was now "home." I ran to her room to see if she was there, to see if she was back from the hospital. But her room was as before, her bed empty, stripped of linen. Slowly it became plain to me that something terribly tragic had happened among us. That harsh morning—the day that Heather left the iron lung behind for her new "home"—is as vivid to me now as it was then, forty-one years ago.

Anonymous

My grief consumes me at times, but I will learn to live with my loss. I cannot forget our son. . . . It seems such a loss for someone as vital as Ron to be gone. When death strikes it is a terrible blow, and the pain is tremendous. I know it takes time to heal a painful wound, especially one affecting your heart. I cannot give up, and I am trying to make my life significant.

Edith Mize, in Death: the Final Stage of Growth, *by Elisabeth Kübler-Ross*

A Tangible Absence

What a blessing, to take the time to integrate loss into our lives so that when a love is lost, our capacity to love is not lost also. From our grief can come growth.

Roy and Jane Nichols, in Death: the Final Stage of Growth, *by Elisabeth Kübler-Ross*

The bereaved often find themselves carrying out actions better suited to the past, perhaps making familiar preparations like setting the table for two people though now they are alone. The incomplete acceptance of the death may lead them, months later, to be subconsciously listening for the accustomed footsteps and sounds of the opening door, for a home-coming which now, they have to painfully remind themselves, cannot be.

John Hinton, Dying

My hand has been on the telephone each time I have wanted to talk to Bill, a hundred times, two hundred times, my finger punching the first three digits until I realize there is no Bill.

Ruth Coughlin, Grieving

One loving Christian couple called or sent flowers on the anniversary of the death of their friend's son, every year for several years. They showed their love by not forgetting.

Billy Graham, Facing Death—and the Life After

Lots of people gain happiness from remembering people who are very special to them, even when they are dead. Just looking at a photograph of a person can bring back memories of when they were alive. This can bring people very close together. . . . When someone has died it can seem very final. They are no longer there for you, but remembering them is part of understanding death and beginning to accept the loss.

Pete Sanders, Death and Dying

Your loved one's personal belongings do not magically disappear with death. Seeing, touching, and smelling your loved one's clothing and other possessions will bring back a flood of feelings. Whether or not you had a positive relationship with your loved one, the feelings may mirror what you are thinking—guilt, loss, anger, reconciliation, or acceptance.

Eva Shaw, What to Do When a Loved One Dies

When my husband died, I don't really remember too much about it. For four or five days, I didn't know who I was or where I was. I didn't know anybody. But when I came out of it and realized what had happened, I really felt awful. It really hit me then, especially when my sons came in and started talking to me—that this was the way it had to be, that this was the way it was.

A widow, in Surviving Grief . . . and Learning to Live Again, *by Dr. Catherine M. Sanders*

Does she want to remember him as he was that morning, or as he is now? That is, does she want to see the body, which may be in mangled form? Most people do want to see the body, regardless of the circumstances, and it can be a very good sign when they do wish to see the body, because this helps them to face the reality of the death.

Rev. Lloyd Beebe, in Death Education: Preparation for Living

Bereavement is a lonely and isolating experience regardless of cause of death.

Arlene Sheskin and Samuel E. Wallace, in Death, Dying, Transcending

Now, after Dave is gone, Joan can sit in his garden and remember the sunny day when friends joined together to say good-bye. She can tend Dave's garden as she tended him, with love and devotion. Together they planted a living, growing memory, bright and beautiful and sweet with the fragrance of life.

Ted Menten, Gentle Closings

When I heard the news that my younger brother had been killed in a car accident, a knot of pain gathered in the pit of my stomach and hardened there. It stayed with me for weeks, even months following his death. The gnawing ache was a constant reminder of his tragic death, and the ragged hole he had left behind.

Anonymous

Really, tears are not a bad sign, you know!
They're Nature's way of helping me to heal.
They relieve some of the stress of sadness.
I know you fear that asking how I'm doing brought this sadness to me.
No, you're wrong, the memory of my son's death will always be with me, only a thought away.

Bereaved parent, in What to Do When a Loved One Dies, *by Eva Shaw*

Strange though it may seem to you, one of the most productive avenues for growth is found through the study and experience of death. . . .

Those who have been immersed in the tragedy of . . . death . . . and who have faced it squarely, never allowing their senses and feelings to become numbed and indifferent, have emerged from their experiences with growth and humanness greater than that achieved through almost any other means.

Elisabeth Kübler-Ross, Death: the Final Stage of Growth

I would like to know if this terrible, terrible ache ever goes away. I really wonder if I can take it. I feel like I'm falling apart and I can't understand why my life had to be this way. You are right. Other people just do not understand.

Grieving widow, in Lifelines, *by Lynn Caine*

Recollections of my mother flow in and out of the days and seasons of my life. It has been twenty-two years since she died. Some memories are warm reminders of her bright spirit. I hear her ready laugh; I smell the lily of the valley talcum powder she used. Other impressions are less comforting—her face haggard with illness, her helpless trembling. Sometimes I even dream about her, and she is always fragile, brittle, like the stiff remains of a dead insect, and I am careful to not hurt her.

Anonymous

I cannot stand the silence. I cannot stand the images playing and replaying before my eyes. Bill sick, Bill dying, Bill in the casket. It is the first time in my life that I can even approach understanding what veterans of war mean when they talk about flashbacks.

Ruth Coughlin, Grieving

A man who had been grief-stricken for weeks after his wife's death said: "What's the point of going on? It's just twenty-four hours of pain. . . . [I] can't get over the fact that I've lost her. People keep on telling me to make a new life, but how can I? There's no future but loneliness and pain." After some sympathetic help, however, he was soon planning how he could manage his home and was inquiring of a family friend if she would keep house for him.

Although mourners have some loyal disinclination to throw off sorrow, they are relieved when grief does ease. As one widow said: "For a day I was my old self again. It was a relief to be happy again and to know that I had not been totally submerged. It still hurt when it all came back, though."

John Hinton, Dying

It is the wind and the rain, O God, the cold and the storm that make this earth of Thine to blossom and bear its fruit. So in our lives it is storm and stress and hurt and suffering that make real men and women bring the world's work to its highest perfection. Let us learn then in these growing years to respect the harder, sterner aspects of life together with its joy and laughter, and to weave them all into the great web which hangs holy to the Lord—Amen.

W. E. B. Du Bois, Prayers for Dark People

CONSOLATION
AND
INSPIRATION

The Power of Hope

I asked God for just one more glimpse of my sister. If only I could see her face in the clouds.

Joy Muschett Banta, recalling the death of her thirteen-year-old sister

Hope is a delicate suffering.

LeRoi Jones, Home: Social Essays

Right now you may want to talk to someone who has traveled his or her grief journey a few miles ahead of you. It really helps to know you are not alone, not "crazy," and not a failure. And if you have misplaced yours for awhile, borrow hope from a friend.

Sandra L. Graves, Ph.D., in What to Do When a Loved One Dies

I am not going to die, I'm going home like a shooting star.

Sojourner Truth

No one can escape death. Then why be afraid of it? In fact, death is a friend who brings deliverance from suffering.

Mohandas Gandhi

When we talk about death, we get in touch with life. Sometimes in our day-to-day routine we get so caught up in doing things that we forget what's really important . . . our beliefs, our dreams, the ones we love. But when we talk about death and, for a moment, confront the fact that we're only here for a little while, we strip away the trappings of our lives and get to the core of what we feel and believe. We become more human as we realize how precious it is to be alive. How wonderful it is if we can share that moment with our children!

Dan Schaefer and Christine Lyons, How Do We Tell the Children?

Death cannot put the brakes on a good dream.

Marva Collins, in "The Most Unforgettable Person in My Family," Ebony, *August 1986*

For the soul of every living thing is in the hand of God, and the breath of all mankind.

Job 12:10, TLB

No, we need not forget our dear loved ones; but we may cling forever to

the enduring hope that there will be a time when we can meet unfettered
and be blessed in that land of everlasting sun where the soul drinks from
the living streams of love that roll by God's high throne.

Dwight L. Moody, Heaven

Hope is some extraordinary spiritual grace that God gives us to control
fears, not to oust them.

Vincent McNabb

I am a poor pilgrim of sorrow,
I'm tossed in this wide world alone,
No hope have I for tomorrow,
I've started to make heav'n my home.
Sometimes I am tossed and driven, Lord,
Sometimes I don't know where to roam,
I've heard of a city called heaven,
I've started to make it my home.

Traditional

Hope arouses, as nothing else can arouse, a passion for the possible.

William Sloan Coffin, Jr.

When Dorothy reached out in the blackness not expecting to find a thing, not even a light switch to shed some hope on her bleak circumstances, she found the hand of Someone right in the midst of her darkest hour. God showed her how to live when he showed her . . . himself.

Joni Eareckson Tada, When Is It Right to Die?

Treasure the memories of past misfortunes; they constitute our bank of fortitude.

Eric Hoffer

We give thanks to God and the Father of our Lord Jesus Christ . . . for the hope which is laid up for you in heaven.

Colossians 1:3, 5, KJV

I still feel loneliness and depression. But I know how to fight my way out; and each time it is easier and I emerge stronger. I still have many anxieties, many fears, but they no longer cripple me. They are no longer the stuff of nightmares. They are problems that can be solved. Somehow. To some degree.

Lynn Caine, Lifelines

Hope and patience are two sovereign remedies for all, the surest reposals, the softest cushions to lean on in adversity.

Robert Burton

Shortly after they gave up on ever having another child and accepted the fact that they would be barren, Joanne got pregnant. Overjoyed, they were now ready to welcome a different baby and allow their dead son a place of his own. . . . Their daughter Trina is now three years old and never became a replacement baby. John and Joanne felt a stronger and deeper love than they had ever imagined was possible.

Dr. Catherine M. Sanders, Surviving Grief . . . and Learning to Live Again

Hope is the thing with feathers that perches in the soul and sings the tune without words and never stops at all.

Emily Dickinson

When I was in Dublin, they were telling me about a father who had lost a little boy. This father had not thought about the future, he had been so entirely taken up with this world and its affairs; but when that little boy, his only child, died, that father's heart was broken, and every night when he returned from work he might be found in his room with his candle and his Bible hunting up all that he could find there about heaven. Some-one asked him what he was doing, and he said he was trying to find out where his child had gone, and I think he was a reasonable man.

Dwight L. Moody, Heaven

The morning my mother went to be with the Lord she kept reaching up . . . she tried to say something about "hand," and Rose didn't know what she wanted. Perhaps, Rose thought, she was trying to say a verse of Scripture, but couldn't get the words out.

"Mother Graham, are you trying to say, 'Father, into Thy hands I commend my spirit'?"

Her hand dropped and a smile came upon her lips. She looked peaceful all day, and once when Rose was about to leave the room, she seemed to yawn. Rose put her arms around her and Mother went to be with her precious Lord.

Billy Graham, Facing Death—and the Life After

Joy Comes in the Morning

I hope the exit is joyful—and I hope never to come back.

Frida Kahlo, in Herrera, Frida Kahlo: The Paintings

Then, of course, there are those who create happiness. They are the people who work diligently to establish an atmosphere that is pleasurable. A widower who spent four years sunk in a pit finally worked himself through to the point where he knew, really knew, things in his life would not change unless he changed them. He set about doing so by going to a local orphanage and inviting all the ten-year-old boys to a football game. For as long as they live those children will probably remember that day.

Harriet Sarnoff Schiff, Living Through Mourning

You will suffer and you will hurt. You will have joy and you will have peace.

Alison Cheek

They that sow in tears shall reap in joy.

Psalm 126:5, KJV

I don't even know how to begin to thank you, and I don't even know how to begin to tell you how sorry I am that this vicious and grotesque killer got you. While the day you died was not a perfect day, . . . it was, however, the day that finally took you out of your pain, for which I am grateful. Rest in peace, pal.

Ruth Coughlin, Grieving

I finally figured out the only reason to be alive is to enjoy it.

Rita Mae Brown

When we think of God's love for us in frightening times, great peace and comfort settle within. When we think of God's care for us, his absolute commitment to our entire well-being, "every trace of terror" can be exiled.

Charles Stanley, A Touch of His Love

In this world, full often, our joys are only the tender shadows which our sorrows cast.

Henry Ward Beecher, Proverbs from a Plymouth Pulpit

I would like to see some kind of encouragement given to people who don't believe in anything beyond this life. I think there has to be a continuation of life in some way. And for me, a continuation of life is being united with God.

Mary Catherine, in Someone You Love Is Dying, *by Martin Shepard, M.D.*

Now is your time of grief, but I will see you again and you will rejoice, and no one will take away your joy.

John 16:22

Sheer joy is [God's], and this demands companionship.

Thomas Aquinas

We each heal at different rates, respond best to different kinds of medicine. My flute had helped bring me back to life.

Diane Cole, After Great Pain

Joy is grief's best music.

Unknown

To those who shall sit here rejoicing, and to those who shall sit here lamenting—greeting and sympathy. So have we done in our time.

Bench inscription, Cornell University

It is not easy. You may place a smile on your face, but your heart will still hurt because your special person is gone. Ultimately you will reach some inner peace, but that is not how it begins: it begins with the attempt.

Harriett Sarnoff Schiff, Living Through Mourning

Unexpected joy is always so keen that . . . it seems to hold enough to reconcile one to the inevitable.

Jessie B. Fremont

Over time, grief gradually changed me. I've come to believe that if we face the many lessons that bereavement offers us, we can finally triumph over sorrow. We have choices over how we will survive our significant losses. We can choose to maintain a bitterly cynical viewpoint, remaining in the conservation/withdrawal phase of grief, or we can confront the lessons of grief, painful as they are, and treat them instead as opportunities for our growth. When we have the courage to do the latter, we have opted for a triumphant survival.

Dr. Catherine M. Sanders, Surviving Grief . . . and Learning to Live Again

Sadness flies away on the wings of time.

Jean de la Fontaine

Weeping may remain for a night, but rejoicing comes in the morning.

Psalm 30:5

Eternal joy is not to be reached by living on the surface. It is rather attained by breaking through the surface, by penetrating the deep things of ourselves, of our world, and of God. The moment in which we reach the last depth of our lives is the moment in which we can experience the joy that has eternity within it, the hope that cannot be destroyed, and the truth on which life and death are built. For in the depth is truth; and in the depth is hope; and in the depth is joy.

Paul Tillich

Birds sing after a storm; why shouldn't people feel as free to delight in whatever remains to them?

Rose Kennedy, Times to Remember

I will turn their mourning into gladness;
I will give them comfort and joy instead of sorrow.

Jeremiah 31:13

The Gift of Friendship

Friendship takes fear from the heart.

Mahabharata

Being a friend means mastering the art of timing. There is a time for silence. A time to let go and allow people to hurl themselves into their own history. And a time to pick up the pieces when it's all over.

Gloria Naylor, The Women of Brewster Place

In the self-help groups that I lead I often hear participants react when someone says, "I just can't seem to move ahead with my life." Others quickly point out improvements they have observed. Someone may say, "You are getting better. I remember the first time I met you; you cried so much that you couldn't even tell us why you were here." Sometimes it takes an outsider to help you see the subtle improvements you have made. Your family and friends may be able to share similar observations that will let you know that you, too, are moving through the process of your grief.

Helen Fitzgerald, The Mourning Handbook

No medicine is more valuable, none more efficacious, none better suited to the cure of all our temporal ills than a friend to whom we may turn for consolation in time of trouble—and with whom we may share our happiness in time of joy.

St. Aelred of Rievaulx, Christian Friendship

I sat by Robert's bed as he lay there, consumed with the pain of cancer. I wanted to help him—read a poem, tell him a funny story, anything to encourage him—but there was nothing much that I could do for my friend. I helped him use the bedpan. I held his hand. And so it went for several hours.

As I left his room I said my good-byes and kissed his gaunt, sallow cheek. Suddenly he gripped my hands and told me that he loved me. It was the first time he had spoken to me that day, and they were his last words to me. I will always treasure those final moments of friendship between us.

Anonymous

Walk beside me, and just be my friend.

Albert Camus

When I do need to talk to someone, I usually talk to Ingrid. She's sort of like a big sister to me. She's sixteen and her father died two years ago, so she's gone through the same thing. She said the first four months are the worst and then it gets easier as it goes along. When my father first died, she came over every day and I told her everything I was feeling. It made me feel better to get it out instead of keeping it inside. It's better sometimes to talk to her instead of my mother because I don't like to make my mother more upset than she already is.

Laurie Marshall, age twelve, in How It Feels When a Parent Dies, *by Jill Krementz*

The person who tries to live alone will not succeed as a human being. His heart withers if it does not answer another heart. His mind shrinks away if he hears only the echoes of his own thoughts and finds no other inspiration.

Pearl S. Buck

Saul and Jonathan—in life they were loved and gracious, and in death they were not parted.

2 Samuel 1:23

The highest privilege there is, is the privilege of being allowed to share another's pain. You talk about your pleasures to your acquaintances; you talk about your troubles to your friends.

Fr. Andrew SDC, Seven Words from the Cross

Grief teaches us that relationships can never be taken for granted. People come into our lives to teach us, and each person is a special gift to be treasured and never taken for granted. Some people seem to be placed into our lives as comforters who help us to get through: special friends, resource people, family members who weren't close or available before. When we finally reach the other side of grief and are on our way to a new life, we may find strangers who become like family. We can only find them if we stay open to other people.

Dr. Catherine M. Sanders, Surviving Grief . . . and Learning to Live Again

When three of Job's friends heard of all the tragedy that had befallen him, they got in touch with each other and traveled from their homes to comfort and console him.

Job 2:11, TLB

At our school they told my class that my father had died, and it sort of made me mad because nobody ever played with me. I guess they were embarrassed. It's hard because they think you're different. . . . It would help if your friends could just play with you and treat you like you're a normal person.

Alletta Laird, age nine, in How It Feels When a Parent Dies

Alone we can do so little; together we can do so much.

Helen Keller

Adjusting to the death of a loved person will always be painful and difficult; many are not helped enough. This may come about through the initial wish of the bereaved to isolate themselves. Later, when they want visitors, friends may avoid the bereaved because they do not know what to say.

John Hinton, Dying

Shared joy is double joy, and shared sorrow is half-sorrow.

Swedish proverb

The people who can share a woman's feelings best are other women. Because . . . they have been there. Some friends are forever. Some are for the moment. Both are to be treasured.

Lynn Caine, Lifelines

A friend is the one who comes in when the whole world has gone out.

Anonymous

Refreshing the Soul

Sun going to shine in my back door some day.

Blues

Last year I looked death in the face and found its lineaments not unkind. But it was not my time. Yet in nature time comes soon and in the fullness of days I shall die, quietly, I trust with my face turned south and eastward; and dream or dreamless I shall death enjoy as I have life.

W. E. B. Du Bois, Autobiography

In the darkest hour the soul is replenished and given strength to continue and endure.

Heart Warrior Chosa

Truth is healing.

Frank Yerby

God gives quietness at last.

John Greenleaf Whittier

Oh, no, I'm not brave. When a thing is certain, there's nothing to be brave about. All you can do is find your consolation.

Agatha Christie, Endless Night

It is only by closing the ears of the soul, or by listening too intently to the clamor of the senses, that we become oblivious of their utterances.

Alexander Crummell

In some ways it's easier for me that my father died the way he did—all of a sudden—instead of having to go through a lot of pain and suffering. The way I think of it is that someone good came down and picked him up because it was his time.

Laurie Marshall, age twelve, in How It Feels When a Parent Dies

I shall be richer all my life for this sorrow! New insights about life have been born. Life is to be lived by striking a line through every minus and turning it into a plus.

Elisabeth Kübler-Ross, Death: The Final Stage of Growth

Inner healing is concerned to bring to light the causes of the inner pain; to help the sufferer to interpret them correctly; and to release the person from the emotional grip of the past.

John Townroe, Christian Spirituality and Healing

Out of suffering have emerged the strongest souls; the most massive characters are seared with scars.

E. H. Chapin

Difficulties are meant to rouse, not discourage. The human spirit is to grow strong by conflict.

William Ellery Channing

Character cannot be developed in ease and quiet. Only through experience of trial and suffering can the soul be strengthened, vision cleared.

Helen Keller

I have set the Lord always before me.
Because he is at my right hand,
I will not be shaken.
Therefore my heart is glad and my tongue rejoices;
my body also will rest secure.

Psalm 16:8-9

Kill the snake of doubt in your soul, crush the worms of fear in your heart and mountains will move out of your way.

Kate Seredy, The White Stag

There are times in everyone's life when something constructive is born out of adversity . . . when things seem so bad that you've got to grab your fate by the shoulders and shake it.

Unknown

For this God is our God for ever and ever,
he will be our guide even to the end.

Psalm 48:14

The Journey to Recovery

Letting Go

I still miss those I loved who are no longer with me, but I find I am grateful for having loved them. The gratitude has finally conquered the loss.

Rita Mae Brown, quoted in When A Friend Dies, *by Marilyn E. Gootman, Ed.D.*

Mourning has its necessities, but there comes a time when it should be done with.

John Hinton, Dying

We all think that kids should grow up and lead full lives. That's what we expect because most of the time that's the way it is. So when children die it doesn't seem fair. But children, being alive, can also die. As difficult as it is to understand, it is also that simple. So we must accept it and begin to heal.

Ted Menten, Gentle Closings

I thought death would be a final leap out of the old tire swing into shimmering Bald Eagle Lake after a final push from long-dead Aunt

Ethel, godmother and childhood pal.

Judith Stoughton, One Woman's Pascal Journey

When someone dies after being sick for a long time, or of old age, it can be easier to accept.

Pete Sanders, Death and Dying

One dies in fire, one dies in water. So do we all belong to death and go to our place.

Togo

Let not the shining thread of hope become so enmeshed in the web of circumstance that we lose sight of it.

Charles W. Chestnutt, Wife of His Youth

A funeral said so much. . . . A great loss had been suffered. I learned to cry at funerals.

Vernon Jarrett

I like remembering my father, but I just don't like crying over him.

Valerie Crowley, age fifteen, in How It Feels When a Parent Dies

The majority of people face dying or the loss of a loved one with courage, even if they do not pretend to understand death.

John Hinton, Dying

Grief melts away
Like snow in May
As if there were no such cold thing.

George Herbert

Hurt and sadness dissipate over time. Thoughts of my loved ones who have gone on usually come and go easily these days. It is such a relief to have pain-free memories in place of the searing recollections of death and loss.

Anonymous

Let us hold up our heads and with firm and steady tread go . . . forward. No one likes to feel that he is continually following a funeral procession.

Booker T. Washington

It was very hard for us to believe that Nicole was really dead. When a child dies that way in an accident, there's no prior warning, not even a hint that your baby's death could be near. It's not like she was sick or anything. We considered having Nicole buried in the traditional way, but my wife and I couldn't go through with it. We had seen children's graves before, some even had gravestones carved as little white lambs. The idea of "visiting" Nicki's plot and seeing a grave marker instead of a growing daughter was just too much for us both. So we decided to have Nicole's body cremated.

Father quoted in Death, Everyone's Heritage, *by Elaine Landau*

Life was meant to be lived, and curiosity must be kept alive. One must never, for whatever reason, turn his back on life.

Eleanor Roosevelt

"Asking Jan to marry me was the most difficult thing I've done—at times it seemed harder than the initial days of grief when I mourned Denise. I wanted to share my life with Jan, but I had a life full of memories with my first wife." Prior to agreeing, Jan and Barry spent six months in counseling. "I'm blessed to have Jan and have her accept that Denise will always be part of our lives."

Eva Shaw, What to Do When a Loved One Dies

Death is not so serious. Pain is.

Andre Malraux, The Human Condition

Just then, Death finished his prowling through the house on his padded feet and entered the room. He bowed to Mama in his way, and she made her manners and left us to act out her ceremonies over unimportant things.

Zora Neale Hurston, Dust Tracks on a Road

Death is a positive reality because it thrusts the issue of meaning upon us. . . . The distinctive claim of the Christian faith is that the meaning of death can ultimately be understood from the perspective of faith in a loving personal God who is known in Jesus Christ.

Richard W. Doss, The Last Enemy

Personal Growth

When we are in pain we cannot comprehend, nor do we wish to, that a rosebud may be carefully carved out of a flaw. That a new life, not better but different, can be carved out by us when we have to deal with the catastrophe of the death of someone special.

Harriet Sarnoff Schiff, Living Through Mourning

Man is a pliable animal, a being who gets accustomed to everything.

Feodor Dostoevsky, The House of the Dead

See, I have refined you, though not as silver;
I have tested you in the furnace of affliction.

Isaiah 48:10

As you work with your grief you can experience new personal growth and a new awareness of the pain and suffering of the people around you. You will find others who are experiencing a loss turning to you for help and comfort, knowing that you are someone who has been or is going through something similar to what they, too, are experiencing.

Helen Fitzgerald, The Mourning Handbook

The wonder is not that the shadows of grief remain. The greater marvel is that eventually some may begin to lift.

Diane Cole, After Great Pain

I have tried to show that there is no simple way to nail "death" into a box, drop it into a slot, and set up a marker. Such a realization may be frustrating, but it is also therapeutic. It can save us from simplistic claims and trivial conclusions.

George M. Schurr, in Death and Ministry

That is why we never give up. Though our bodies are dying, our inner strength in the Lord is growing every day. These troubles and sufferings of ours are, after all, quite small and won't last very long. Yet this short time of distress will result in God's richest blessing upon us forever and ever!

2 Corinthians 4:16-17, TLB

If afflictions refine some, they consume others.

Thomas Fuller, Gnomologia

I wish that this had never happened to you and your friend, but it did. There is nothing you can do to change what has happened, but there is much you can do to help yourself. I have gone through what you are going through now. I know people your age whose friends have died. I can make this promise: You will grow from this tragedy. You will learn more about yourself and others. You will become more sensitive. Your view of the world will change.

Marilyn E. Gootman, Ed.D., When a Friend Dies

I like living. I have sometimes been wildly, despairingly, acutely miserable, racked with sorrow, but through it all I still know quite certainly that just to be alive is a grand thing.

Agatha Christie

Never does one feel oneself so utterly helpless as in trying to speak comfort for great bereavement. I will not try it. Time is the only comforter for the loss of a mother.

Jane Welsh Carlyle

I have passed through the Red Sea, the wilderness, and the valley of the shadow of death, and I can see my way clear to the Promised Land.

Anonymous

All sorrows can be borne if you put them into a story or tell a story about them.

Isak Dinesen

For some a clearer understanding of death will result in a greater appreciation of life. Acknowledging the certainty that life is a finite experience may encourage us to live our lives as fully as possible.

Elaine Landau, Death, Everyone's Heritage

And I am stronger, strong enough to face loneliness. When it strikes now, I understand that it is a sign that I am going through a time of growth, of change. Growth is a lonely task, and when one feels the very sands of life shifting under one's feet, it is frightening. But in time, one adjusts to the new—the new situation, the new woman, the wiser me— and loneliness disappears.

Lynn Caine, Lifelines

He who wants to enjoy the glory of the sunrise must live through the night.

Anonymous

Choosing to see the funny side as well as the serious side of life heals our pain and encourages wellness. Because it is habit-forming and contagious, laughter shared with others can heal them as well as ourselves.

Dr. Catherine M. Sanders, Surviving Grief . . . And Learning to Live Again

No life is so hard that you can't make it easier by the way you take it.

Ellen Glasgow

And I am sure that God who began the good work within you will keep right on helping you grow in his grace until his task within you is finally finished on that day when Jesus Christ returns.

Philippians 1:6, TLB

A New Life

A few days ago my mother asked me how I would feel if another man liked her and she liked him and they got married. I said as long as they're happy it was okay but that there'd never be a father like my father.

Laurie Marshall, age twelve, in How It Feels When a Parent Dies

Is life a pregnancy? That would make death a birth.

Florida Scott-Maxwell, "The Measure of My Days"

A funeral helps people face up to life.

Pete Sanders, Death and Dying

Those who lose something or someone very precious to them seldom fully recover. They don't get over it—they just get used to it.

Janice Harris Lord, Beyond Sympathy

There is no better time to talk about the living than when we remember the dead.

Chinua Achebe, Things Fall Apart

If your husband died and you always spent your birthday in your home surrounded by those you love, change the setting. Perhaps hold the gathering at an adult child's home or a restaurant. You will still feel his absence, certainly, but it need not permeate all you are doing and any pleasure you might find.

Harriet Sarnoff Schiff, Living Through Mourning

The unendurable is the beginning of the curve of joy.

Djuna Barnes, Nightwood

What do we live for, if it is not to make life less difficult for each other?

George Eliot

Suffering passes: having suffered never passes.

Jean Péguy

We cannot find peace if we are afraid of the windstorms of life.

Elisabeth Kübler-Ross, To Live Until We Say Goodbye

Grief teaches us that we need to keep reaching out to others, to get a new set of people when we find our own set growing smaller. If we do this, we will never be lonely or feel excluded from life.

Catherine M. Sanders, Surviving Grief . . . And Learning to Live Again

I didn't need all that ritual and all of that sobbing around the graveside. In retrospect the fact that the body was destroyed also makes it easier for me to accept the finality of death. It's better than thinking of some little spot where he's buried.

Widow, in Death as a Fact of Life, *by David Hendin*

In time, you will feel better than you do now. But for now, try to be patient with yourself. You've been through a lot.

Janice Harris Lord, Beyond Sympathy

No one would ever choose to grow because of the death of a friend. But now that it has happened to you, what can you do to make meaning out of your experience? Think about that in the weeks, months, and years ahead. You will find a way. . . . Talk with others, write, draw, listen to music, or plant a tree in memory of your friend. Many people find that reaching out to others, doing good deeds, and making the world a better place can help them to heal from the death of a friend.

Marilyn E. Gootman, Ed.D., When a Friend Dies

Take time to recall and rejoice in the progress you've made since that moment when someone you loved died. Call back the memories of the good times and the great times. And if there were trying, soul-wrenching and horrifying times, perhaps as you witnessed your loved one slowly, even painfully move to the final transition to death, put these experiences in among the many displayed in your own kaleidoscope of life.

Eva Shaw, What to Do When a Loved One Dies

We are healed of a suffering only be experiencing it to the full.

Marcel Proust

An Enduring Faith

We need not give way to defiance, or rejection, or fear, or any of the other attitudes people adopt in the face of the reality of death. There is another way—the way of Christ—by which we know that while the experience of death is certain, so also is the fact of heaven. For the Christian, death can be faced realistically and with victory.

Billy Graham, Facing Death—and the Life After

Before the ship of your life reaches its last harbor, there will be long drawn-out storms, howling and jostling winds, and tempestuous seas that make the heart stand still. If you do not have a deep and patient faith in God, you will be powerless to face the delay, disappointment, and vicissitudes that inevitably come. . . . In the spirit of the darkness, we must not despair, we must not become bitter—we must not lose faith.

Martin Luther King, Jr., Strength to Love

Faith is a bridge across the gulf of death.

Edward Young

The Christian's response to bereavement includes both grief and hope.

Schuyler P. Brown, in Death and Ministry

We do not want you to be ignorant about those who fall asleep, or to grieve like the rest of men, who have no hope. We believe that Jesus died and rose again and so we believe that God will bring with Jesus those who have fallen asleep in him.

1 Thessalonians 4:13-14

If it can be verified, we don't need faith. . . . Faith is for that which lies on the other side of reason. Faith is what makes life bearable, with all its tragedies and ambiguities and sudden, startling joys.

Madeleine L'Engle, Walking on Water: Reflections on Faith & Art

Faith is necessary to victory.

William Hazlitt

Know therefore that the Lord your God is God; he is the faithful God, keeping his covenant of love to a thousand generations of those who love him and keep his commands.

Deuteronomy 7:9

If God takes note of each humble sparrow—who they are, where they are, and what they're doing—I know he keeps tabs on me.

Joni Eareckson Tada, When Is It Right to Die?

God's promises are anchors for your soul. They keep you grounded in his love and faithfulness, reminding you of your dependence on him. What God promises, he will fulfill.

Charles Stanley, A Touch of His Love

Faith is not a storm cellar to which men and women can flee for refuge from the storms of life. It is, instead, an inner force that gives them the strength to face those storms and their consequences with serenity of spirit.

Sam J. Earvin, Jr.

We know these things are true by believing, not by seeing.

2 Corinthians 5:7, TLB

God was merciful. Had he lived my son would have been incapacitated eventually. He would have been one of those who sit looking out the window while other children play. There was no surgery that could help him back then and he died. God spared him the pain of being a looker-on at life. Although we miss him and it certainly hurts us that he is not here, we are also thankful that he was spared a life of pain.

Bereaved parent, in Living Through Mourning

The only way to meet affliction is to pass through it solemnly, slowly, with humility and faith, as the Israelites passed through the sea. Then its very waves of misery will divide, and become to us a wall, on the right side and on the left, until the gulf narrows before our eyes, and we land safe on the opposite shore.

Dinah Maria Mulock

You will find after a while that the good days come more frequently and the bad ones start to decline, both in number and in intensity. After all, there is nothing written in the stars that says you can't be a happy person again. Much as you loved that person or those persons who died, you don't have to wear black for the rest of your life!

Helen Fitzgerald, The Mourning Handbook

You build in darkness if you have faith. When the light returns you have made of yourself a fortress which is impregnable to certain kinds of trouble; you may even find yourself needed and sought by others as a beacon in their dark.

Olga Rosmanith

The life of faith always contains risk and more often than not will create a sense of insecurity . . . [Yet] the claim of Christian hope is that we will someday know even as we now are known (1 Cor. 13:12), and that experience holds the promise of a full and complete relationship with God.

Richard W. Doss, The Last Enemy

I am, after all, a friend of Jesus. And where he is, there I too am to be. Is he not alive? Then I too am to live, and death shall not separate me from the love of God.

Helmut Thielicke, Death and Life

Joy is the serious business of heaven.

C. S. Lewis, The Joyful Christian

I heard a loud shout from the throne saying, "Look, the home of God is now among men, and he will live with them and they will be his people; yes, God himself will be among them. He will wipe away all tears from their eyes, and there shall be no more death, nor sorrow, nor crying, nor pain. All of that has gone forever."

Revelation 21:3-4, TLB